HISTORIC
PUBLISHING

2015
"Dedicated to the accurate and
Historical integrity of classic works"

The Heir of Slaves:
An Autobiography
By
William Pickens
[b. 1881]

THE HEIR OF SLAVES

AN AUTOBIOGRAPHY

BY

WILLIAM PICKENS

Professor in Talladega College, Alabama.

THE PILGRIM PRESS
BOSTON NEW YORK CHICAGO

The Heir of Slaves

THE RUMFORD PRESS
CONCORD *N*H*U*S*A

The Heir of Slaves

CONTENTS

The Heir of Slaves

FOREWORD

IT IS a common story; there were more than three million slaves; there are perhaps ten million heirs born of the slaves since 1865. What reason can there be for writing a story which is so common?

One reason is that some want to know the story, and have asked for it. These several requests have been prompted, perhaps, by no expectation of anything wonderful in the story, but by the fact that it is common and can therefore stand as the representative of the class. This last reason is the one that emboldens me to the task. The interests of a class may justify the examination and description of a typical specimen.

I shall therefore regard myself as speaking to friends. I shall not aim to evaluate the thing I say, but I shall simply relate the incidents and leave the worth of them to the judgment of the audience. If I am frank, it is only to be true. Such a story could have no self-glory and little expectation of applause.

THE HEIR OF SLAVES

I. MY PARENTAGE

I WAS born on the 15th day of January, 1881, according to the recollection of my parents. There was no record of the sixth child, for the sixth baby in no novelty in a family. But as the historian finds the dates of old battles by the comets and eclipses, so can we approximate this event by an impressive happening: because of the martyrdom of a good President I narrowly escaped the honor of being named *Garfield* Pickens.

With natural and pardonable curiosity people have often asked me about my parentage, and if I knew anything about my ancestry. My immediate parents I know, and have known something of one or two of my grandparents. But about any ancestry more remote than this all that I can know is that it seems natural and logical to conclude by analogy and induction that I probably had some additional forbears. Most of the negroes in the United States who are as many as thirty years old have no reliable knowledge of ancestry beyond perhaps their grandparents. The family tree is just sprouting or just beginning to put forth shoots. How the causes of this inhered in the system of slavery is well known. There are good and sensible reasons for keeping an ancestral record of certain breeds of horses, but little reason for keeping that of slaves, simply because the worth of a man depends less upon the value and blood of his father than does the price of a horse.

Three-fourths of all the negroes I have ever seen had other blood. Sometimes times it was not visible in their faces: the blackest man may have a mulatto grandmother on his mother's side. And your average brown negro - if all the different sorts of blood in his veins should get at war with each other, the man would blow up like a stick of dynamite.

My father in color and hair is African although his features are not prominently African, and I knew one of his sisters who was brown. My mother's mother, who lived long in our family and "raised" all of the grandchildren, was a characteristic little

African woman, vivacious and longlived, with a small head and keen eyes. She could thread her own needles when she was eighty years of age. She lived for forty years with a broken back, the upper part of her body being carried in a horizontal position, at right angles to her lower limbs, so that she must support her steps with a staff if she walked far. This was one of the results of slavery. Being a high-tempered house-servant in that system she had been beaten and struck across the back with a stick. Even in her old age her temper rose quick, but was volatile, and she was a very dear and most helpful grandmother. My mother's father, whom I never saw, and who perhaps died a slave, was half Cherokee Indian, his father being a Cherokee. I suppose that his other half was negro, since he was married in slavery to my grandmother.

My mother was an average-sized brown woman, whose features were somewhat modified by her Indian strain and whose hair was black and of a negro-Indian texture. She was simply famous for the amount of hard work she could do. As a cook she could get a breakfast in the shortest possible time; as a washerwoman she could put out the clothes of a large family by noon. And her work must have been well done, for she could never supply the demand for her services, and she died of overwork at the age of about forty-five. I was the sixth of her ten children.

My birthplace was in Anderson County, South Carolina, near Pendleton, in a rural neighborhood called "over the river," where lies the first dim, flickering memory of the humble estate to which I was born. My parents were farmers of the tenant or day-labor class and were ever on the move from cabin to cabin, with the proverbial unacquisitiveness of the "rolling stone." They were illiterate, but were beginning to learn to read the large-print New Testament sold by the book agents. That part of the state was exceedingly poor, with red hills and antiquated agriculture. From such sections of the old South the immigration agent of the West easily induced many negroes to cross the Mississippi into debt-slavery. My parents were industrious but improvident, and began early to talk of moving to Arkansas where the soil was fertile and wages high. This was possible only by allowing some Western farmer to pay the fares of the family through his agent, and by signing a contract to work on that farmer's land until the debt was paid according to that farmer's reckoning.

The earliest family moving which I remember was from "over the river" to "Price's place," which makes my memory reach back to my second year. At "Price's" there was our one-room cabin on a small hill facing the larger hill on which stood the "great house" of the landowner. I remember the curiosity of our first clock, an "eight-day" specimen, which my father immediately took to pieces and put together again; and he still boasts that his clock has never been to the repair shop. Here, too, I received the first impression of my personal appearance. I had a large head, for a certain comical minded uncle would play frightened whenever I came near him, and he dubbed that part of my anatomy "a wag'n-body."

After a year or so we moved from "Price's" to "Clark's place," nearer Pendleton. Here I received my first slight acquaintance with the English alphabet, which I learned so readily that my sisters took delight in leading me to school with them, although I must have been at least two years under school age. It was a characteristic negro schoolhouse built of logs, with one door and one window, the alatter having no panes and being closed by a board shutter which swung on leather hinges outward. The house was not larger then a comfortable bedroom and had a "fire-place" opposite the door. The children faced the fireplace, so that the scant light fell through the door upon their books. There were no desks; the seats were long board benches with no backs. The teacher insisted that the students sit in statuesque postures, not moving a limb too often. Persuasion to study and good deportment consisted of a hickory switch, a cone-shaped paper "dunce cap" and a stool on which the offender must stand on one foot for an enormous length of time. Although I had readily learned my elements under sympathetic tutelage at home, about all I remember of this first schooling is the menacing words of the teacher, the movements of that switch and the astonishing balancing acts of the dunce cap wearers. The chief fountain of academic knowledge in such schools was the famous old "blue-back speller." After leaving the nonsense syllables in the beginning of that book, the milestones of attainment were first the page of dissyllables beginning with "baker" and secondly the page of polysyllables containing "compressibility." A person interested in your advancement might ask first had you "got to 'baker' yet," and secondly could you spell "compressibility."

After a year at "Clark's place" we moved to Pendleton, and from that time till I reached the age of eighteen I can count no less than twenty removals of our family.

The motives that carried my mother and father from the country into the little town of Pendleton were more than good; they were sacred. It was a consideration for the future of their children. Having lived nearer town for a year, they learned that the houses, the wages and the schools of the village were superior to those of the country. The country school was poorly housed and still more poorly taught. Its sessions lasted for only a few hot weeks of summer after the "laying by" of the crops, and for a few cold weeks of winter between the last of harvest and the time for clearing the fields. School interests were secondary to farm interests; the raising of children must not interfere with the raising of cotton. The landowner would not tolerate a tenant who put his children to school in the farming seasons. In the town, my mother had cooked and washed, in the country she had been a field hand. A cook has somewhat better opportunities to care for small children; there was a story of how Mother, returning from field work to the railfence where she had laid the baby to sleep, found a great snake crawling over the child. In the country my father worked while another man reckoned.

It always took the whole of what was earned to pay for the scant "rations" that were advanced to the family, and at settlement time there would be a margin of debt to keep the family perennially bound to a virtual owner. A man in town who ran a bar and hotel, and who needed help, offered to pay this margin of debt and bring the whole family to town if Father would be his man of all work and Mother a cook. Wages were small but paid promptly, and there was no binding debt. They went, as one instinctively moves from a greater toward a lesser pain. There was one certain advantage; the children obtained six months instead of six weeks of schooling.

My parents were always faithful members of the Baptist church, and even while my father was hotel man and "bartender," he was superintendent of the Sunday school of his village church. Had he been keeping bar for himself he would have been excommunicated by his brethren. An inevitable, but not inalterable, dual moral system has grown up in the inter-racial life of the South; a negro may be tolerated by his own race in doing for a white man what would not meet with toleration if done for himself; and a white man may be excused by his own race if he does to a negro what would be instantaneously condemned if done to a white man.

Twenty odd years ago Pendleton was a characteristic little town of the older South. There was the central public "square" on one side of which stood the "calaboose" and on the opposite side the post office. It was full of politics and whisky, but withal there was extraordinary good feeling between the white and the black race. The employer of my father was the head man of the village, whom the people called "town councilor," a position corresponding to the mayoralty in larger towns. This man was a boon companion of my father, and they ran the town together. Race antagonism seemed not to touch our world. I can remember many things which indicate that race feeling was not nearly as combustible in Pendleton then as it is in most places now. For example, on Christmas Day the black folk used to say that "there is no law for Christmas." And so the young negro men, in a good natured spree, would catch the lone policeman, who was always more a joke than a terror, and lock him in the calaboose to stay a part of Christmas Day, while one of the black men with star and club would strut about the town and play officer - an act for laughter then, but which now would summon the militia from the four quarters of almost any state and be heralded the world over as ugly insurrection.

For some reason at this period wages were steadily declining in the older states of the South. In 1887 the wage for doing a day's work or picking a hundred pounds of cotton in the fields was thirty-five or forty cents. The Western immigration agent was busy telling of glorious opportunities beyond the Mississippi, and many minds among black people were being turned in that direction. After several years of village life, and after engaging in various employments, including another year of farming, we moved to Seneca, S. C. Father had been in turn farmer, hotel man, section hand, brakeman and fireman.

In these awakening years, when the mind is supposed to receive so much, I had about two short terms of schooling so poor that in New England it would not be called schooling at all. My mother's constant talk and ambition was to get an opportunity "to school the children." One of the chief causes of the rapid advancement of the negro race since the Civil War has been the ambition of emancipated black mothers for the education of their children. Many an educated negro owes his enlightenment to the toil and sweat of a mother.

But "hard times" and the immigration agent were fast persuading my father to risk the future of his family in the malarial swamp-lands of Arkansas.

II. TO ARKANSAS

AT last an agent representing a planter in the Mississippi River Valley of Arkansas induced my father to sign a contract to move his entire family to that state. In order to appreciate the persuasions which the agent used, the ignorance and superstition of such families would have to be understood. Ignorant people are too quick to believe tales of other places and other times. Our family had a hundred "signs," mostly signs of evil. By the ruddy glow of the fire at nights the children were told of ghosts, of strange cats, dogs, voices and sounds, of the "no-headed man," of graveyards, and the weird history of the ill-famed "three-mile bottom" near the village. The Federal soldiers were described not as common men, but as beings from a super-world; and with the irony of truth Lincoln was pictured as more than mortal.

To such a group reports from the outside world come with a feeling of otherworldliness. The agent said that Arkansas was a tropical country of soft and balmy air, where cocoanuts, oranges, lemons and bananas grew. Ordinary things like corn and cotton, with little cultivation, grew an enormous yield.

On the 15th of January, 1888, the agent made all the arrangements, purchased tickets, and we boarded the train in Seneca, S. C., bound toward Atlanta, Ga. Our route lay through Birmingham and Memphis, and at each change of trains there seemed to be some representative of the scheme to see us properly forwarded, like so much freight billed for we knew not where. It was midwinter, but with all the unquestioning faith and good cheer of our race we expected to land at the other end of our journey in bright sunshine and spring weather.

And a comical-looking lot we must have been. We had no traveling cases, but each one bore some curious burden - sacks of clothes, quilts, bags, bundles and baskets. When we left our home the weather was comparatively mild, but as fate would have it, the nearer we got to Arkansas, the colder it became. In Memphis the snow was deep and the wind biting. The faith and

17

enthusiasm of the party grew less; perhaps the older heads were waking up to a suspicion. The further we got from our South Carolina home, the dearer it seemed, as is true of most things in their first abandonment.

When we reached a small station in Arkansas, like freight again we were met by two double-team wagons of the unknown planter to whom we were consigned. We were hauled many miles through cypress "brakes" and snow and ice sufficiently thick to support the teams. The older people, I suppose, had by this time comprehended the situation, but we children were constantly peering out from under our quilts and coverings, trying to discover a cocoanut or an orange blossom, while the drivers swore at the mules for slipping on the solid ice. Perhaps nothing could equal this disappointment unless it be the chagrin of those ignorant negroes who have been induced to go to Africa under the persuasion that bread trees grew there right on the brink of molasses ponds, and wild hogs with knives and forks sticking in their backs trotted around ready baked!

When we reached the estate of our consignee, still like freight we were stored away, bags, bundles, boxes and all of us, in a one-room hut to await the breaking of winter and the beginning of field work.

What could we do? The planter had the contract binding us hard and fast. Just what we owed for transportation no one knew; besides we had been furnished with salt meat, meal and molasses for the first weeks of enforced idleness, and we were supplied with a little better food, including sugar, coffee and flour, when field work began. As in the case of any property on which one has a lease, our lessor could lay out more on our maintenance in the seasons when we were bringing returns.

When the first year's settlement came around, and a half hundred bales of cotton had been produced by the family and sold by the planter, Father came home with sad, far-away eyes, having been told that we were deeper in debt than on the day of our arrival. And who could deny it? The white man did all the

18

reckoning. The negro did all the work. The negro can be robbed of everything but his humor, and in the bottom lands of Arkansas he has made a rhyme. He says that on settlement day the landowner sits down, takes up his pen and reckons thus:

"A nought's a nought, and a figger's a figger -
All fer de white man - none fer de nigger!"

But we were not long depressed. To keep down debts in the ensuing winter Mother cooked and washed and Father felled trees in the icy "brakes" to make rails and boards. No provisions were drawn from the planter. The old debt remained, of course, and perhaps took advantage of this quiet period to grow usuriously. This low land is malarial, chills and fevers returning like the seasons. Our medicine and physician, too, had to be secured on the feudal plan, the planter paying the bills. Under such a system the physician has the greatest possible temptation to neglect the patient; his pay is sure, and there is no competition. The spring sickness was miserable; we had come from an elevated, healthy country, and our constitutions fell easy prey to the germs of the lowlands.

For the first year the children were kept out of school in hope of getting rid of the debt. Very small children can be used to hoe and pick cotton, and I have seen my older sisters drive a plow. The next year we attended the short midsummer and midwinter sessions of the plantation school. The school was dominated by the interests of the planter; when the children were needed in the fields he simply commanded the school to close. It was an old-fashioned district school, where the spelling classes stood in line with recognized "head" and "foot." Your ability to spell was denoted by your position in the line relative to the "head" and the "foot." When your neighbor toward the head missed a word and you spelled it, you "turned him down" with all others who had missed that word in succession, that is, you took your position above them. If you were absent from a class, when you returned, whatever had been your position in the line, you had to "go foot." I had a sister a year or so older than I, who stood "head" about all of the time, while I stood second; and we

19

used to stay home a day for the exquisite pleasure of going foot and turning the whole class down. This sister had a phenomenal memory when a child.

The second year the whole family plunged into work, and made a bigger and better crop. But at reckoning time history repeated itself; there was still enough debt to continue the slavery. If the debt could not be paid in fat years, there was the constant danger that lean years would come and make it bigger. But there was the contract - and the law; and the law would not hunt the equity, but would enforce the letter of the contract. It was understood that the negro was unreliable, and the courts must help the poor planters.

There was but one recourse - the way of escape. The attempt must be executed with success, or there might be fine and peonage. On some pretext my father excused himself and went to Little Rock. A few miles out of that city he found a landowner who would advance the fares for the family and rent to us a small farm. This looks at first sight like "jumping from the frying-pan into the fire," but a rented farm with a definite loan is a different proposition from a state of debt-slavery, where the creditor sells all the produce and does all the counting. Moreover, when a condition is about as bad as it can be, there is a tendency in human nature to move on to another bad condition with a sort of desperate venture. Human nature will flee from a known condition that is very bad to an unknown condition that might be worse, in spite of Lord Hamlet's soliloquy. And so one night the young children and some goods were piled into a wagon and the adults went afoot. By morning we were in the town of Augusta, twelve or fifteen miles away, where we caught the first train.

I have one very pleasant recollection of the place from which we had escaped. An aged negro, a characteristic Uncle Remus, would come some nights and relate to us quaint animal stories. The antics and cleverness of "Bre'r Rabbit Bre'r Bar, Bre'r Fox, Sis' Cow and Bre'r Tommy Mud Turtle" did much to enliven the dullness of the hours.

III. BEGINNING SCHOOL IN EARNEST

THE desperate move to Galloway, in the neighborhood of Little Rock, was by no means an unlucky one. For one whole year, of course, we children were kept out of school to clear up the new debt. The debt was paid. Meanwhile my mother heard that in the city of Little Rock and in the town Argenta, across the river from Little Rock, there were nine months' term of school. Think of it! Nine months of schooling for the children.

We moved to Argenta in the winter of 1890-91. This move cityward was not prompted, as is usually charged in such cases, by any desire to get away from work, but by the high motives of education and the future. The prospect struck me with so much force that I set to work and learned to write before I could be sent to school. I could not enter at once - work had to be done and means gotten so that we could start in the fall of 1891. All members of the family worked ceaselessly, about the homes in the city and on the farms near the city. While running errands and making fires at a certain hotel I saw and recognized the face of a quack doctor, a man with long hair, who had once come through the bottom lands from which we had escaped and had frightened my mother out of all her ready cash for his cure-all medicines by telling her that I had consumption. Mentioning the incident to him, "Are you the man?" asked I, with boyish frankness. And he, with quack-doctor frankness, replied, "That depends, my boy, upon whether the medicine helped or hurt you, and upon whether you would like to buy some more."

The Argenta schools opened in September. We could not attend regularly in the weeks that preceded Christmas, for we were at work picking cotton in the neighboring fields. It took the energies of the whole family to get a start. My attendance before Christmas was for only a few scattering days. After Christmas, however, I started in school not to miss another day during that school year - not to miss another day for the next seven years' school years - and indeed not to miss another unnecessary day until I had finished at Yale in 1904.

This was my real start in school, and I was now nearly eleven years old. As a peaceful country boy I was at first imposed upon, but one fine day I laid aside my unwarlike habits and became sufficiently belligerent to win the respect of a certain class of my fellows. I had to fight my way on the playground as well as in the classroom, and at the same time I had to render my accounts and make my peace with the stern government of a teacher who was a fine instructor and a severe disciplinarian - just the proper governor for such a rebellious little state as a city public school. I remember how at the end of that school year he called me out, with his brows lowering as if a storm was going to break, and sternly commanded me to take my seat on the bench in front of his desk - the well known judgment seat where many a little sinner had been called to a sure, even if a reluctant, repentance. I began mentally to review my day's record in order to anticipate the accusation, when he with the same sternness of voice began to pronounce, "This boy" - then hesitating and transfixing me with his terrible eye - "entered school three months late, started behind everybody else, and now he's the leader of his class!"

This teacher's name was J. S. Pleasant, and although he was very strict, the name is not at all inapplicable to his general character. He was my teacher for the following four years. Very often when the teacher had passed a question or a problem around to all the rest of the class and they had failed to answer or to solve it, he would say, "Well, 'Always Ready' will take it" - which was a nickname he sometimes applied to me.

In a personal history I might be expected to tell about my school career and record. In mathematics I never received less than 100 per cent. as a daily average, and only once did I make less than 100 per cent. on an examination in that subject. I state this fact because so many men and women of the white race have asked me particularly how I fared in the subject of mathematics.

I committed my lessons to memory. The lessons in physiology and history I learned verbatim every day, so that I could repeat them, just as they were written, with as much ease as I can say the Lord's Prayer. When I reached the high school we had a large book known as "Barnes's General History." The lessons were from five to ten pages, and I had acquired the ability to commit them by reading them three times over. This I did every day. The history teacher at the end of the year who, after having me stand and recite the last lesson verbatim, said, "I never believed that he would go through this whole book in that way." For the last few minutes of each recitation during the year she had asked me to rise and go through the whole lesson, as in declamation. She would then question me, evidently to see if I knew the *parts* as well as the *whole*. Any question in the lesson would be answered; I had not learned by sound merely.

I was deeply in love with school and study. Very often I reached the schoolhouse before the janitor arrived. From the nickels and dimes which I received for errands and small jobs I would save sufficient money to buy my books. When I was attending the grammar school my mother endeavored one day to keep me at home to draw water for the washing. She never tried it again - I cried and pleaded as if my heart would burst. The prospect of missing my classes for a day seemed to me absolutely unbearable. It seemed that it would tear down all that I had builded. My mother seized a switch to chastize me, but when she listened to my words and looked into my face she saw that it was not rebellion, and with a rather satisfied laugh she said that I might go, if I was that "crazy" about school. I can see now that she was rather proud of the event, for never again did she make any arrangement that would keep me out of school for a day. The whole family came to regard my attendance at school as a foregone conclusion. The children called me "old man," because I would not play until after I had learned my lessons. These were almost invariably learned before sundown. At the end of that very year I received from the teacher a prize for being "never absent, never tardy." It was a book entitled "Our Manners and Social Customs," and it was the first book outside of a school text that I had ever read.

The opportunity which a mother's pride created for my schooling during her life could not continue after her death. She died of overwork and consequent broken health. She had been determined to keep her children in school and had worked from early morning till late at night to that end. We seldom waked early enough to catch a glimpse of her, and before her return at night sleep had weighed down the eyelids of the younger children.

I had just entered upon my fourth year in the city school when my mother died in October. Imagine, if you can, the sorrow and confusion, amounting almost to dismay, that filled the heart and mind of a boy of thirteen, who was ambitious and who knew that his mother was the mainstay of his education and his future - a boy who loved school as dearly as any other boy ever loved a gun or a motor-cycle. I knew what my mother had meant to the family and that without her it would be impossible for my father to keep all the children in school. It was her love and ambition, I knew, that had given me the high privilege of study, and without her I could not be certain of my daily bread for the school year on which we had just entered.

But the ways of Providence are inscrutable, and this confusion and predicament thrust upon me a blessing. I secured a place to earn my board by rising at four o'clock in the morning and also working after school hours until seven o'clock in the evening - and I got my lessons just as well, or better than ever before. Out of misfortune and a hard situation I had to pluck independence.

In this temporary confusion one thought was of more permanent help to me than all other things. Mother had taught us to believe in God, and I reasoned that God would not cause such a good mother to begin such a good work and then remove that mother without intending that in some other way that work was to go on. The thought led me on and on to a greater and greater faith in my opportunities.

IV. A SKIFF-FERRY SCHOOL BOY

IN THE following year I became a ferryman on the Arkansas River to support myself during the last year of the grammar school. The grammar school at that time completed the ninth year, the high school adding three years more.

The town of Argenta, which for a brief space bore the appellation of North Little Rock, is situated, as the latter name implies, on the left bank of the Arkansas River opposite the City of Little Rock. In the early '90's Argenta was famed as one of the worst places in the United States; debauchery, blood and murder were no uncommon spectacles. The incoming traveler shrugged his shoulders when he heard the name "Argenta."

At that time there were only two railroad bridges, adapted also for foot and wagon passage; and all passers had to pay toll, the foot fare per capita being five cents. This condition gave rise to another industry, carried on chiefly by negro men, that of a "skiff ferry." These small boats in which the boatman uses two oars and sits with his back towards the fore, were used to row passengers over the Arkansas to and from Argenta to the foot of Main Street in Little Rock. The fare had been five cents, but under the stress of competition it had become by this time five cents for the round trip. There were about a dozen skiffmen earning each from two to three dollars a day. I quickly mastered all this ferry-craft, sometimes rowing a boat myself and sometimes working as a second oarsman, assisting one of the men. My average wage was about forty cents a day. When I rowed a boat alone I received more; when I rowed as an assistant my pay was at the mercy of the principal, and he paid me according to his earnings or his fancy. I was soon as good an oarsman as any man I worked with, but I was only a school boy, fourteen years of age, and no one would think of paying me a man's wages even for a man's work. But the pittance was saving me my education and my future; and boy although I was, I looked at the present circumstance in the light of the future, and never thought that the condition was too hard, but only the high price of a valuable possession.

This river work also profited me physically; the use of two oars is conducive to symmetry of body, and there is no danger of the one-sided development which Ben Hur dreaded from the one-oar method of the Roman galley. There had been some family doubts about the soundness of my constitution, after the hard wear in the bottom lands of Arkansas, but this ferry work remade my shoulders and chest and lungs. During the school year I could row on Saturdays, and could get a boat by myself on Sundays and work until Sunday school time and afterwards.

I worked again on the ferry in the summer of 1896, and any ferryman was glad to have my services, as I was an able oarsman and also a hustler in securing passengers.

During the summer of 1896 a new problem was before me for solution in reference to my education. I had entered the Argenta school five years before, knowing nothing save to read and spell simple words and to write in my self-taught style. I had not missed a day or an hour of school since that first year, and I had led all of my classes all of the time. The grammar school course was now completed and to stop seemed a calamity. There was no high school in the district and no accessible private school; besides, I could not pay for private instruction. There was a High School in Little Rock to which students from our side of the river could not go except by special permission of the school authorities, and only then by paying two dollars and fifty cents per month. I could not have much hope of getting into this school, but against the bare possibility I saved my earnings on the ferry, bought none of the things which would please a boy of fifteen years, and came to the end of the summer with about forty dollars in a savings bank, practically every cent that I had earned.

There was one fortunate circumstance: the principal of the Argenta school was a boarder in the home of the principal of the Little Rock High School and had constantly praised me as a student. Some days before the opening of school I was called to the home of the High School principal to take the entrance examinations. I have heard him say since that in each of the subjects of arithmetic, grammar, United States history and spelling I was marked 100 per cent., and that especially in the subject of arithmetic he had looked up "catch" problems to test the value of my former principal's praises. However that may be, when I went to register at the offices of the Board of Education, I was not too minutely questioned as to the "residence of parents," etc., the superintendent taking no seeming notice of the fact that I was from over the river. And when I reached the secretary's desk in the line of applicants and received my certificate of entrance to the High School of Little Rock, what a critical moment was passed, what a vista was opened for me! Three more years of schooling were assured. I could work on the ferry in summer and at week-ends to buy necessary books and clothing. I plunged into that High School work with a zest such as I have seldom experienced since. My never-absent, never-tardy record was maintained, and indeed during the three High School years only once was I absent, and then because of an illness that took me for a day in the spring of my last year.

When I entered the High School the class had had a beginners' algebra for one year, and were now taking up the more advanced book. I had never studied that subject, but at the end of the first month or so I was ranked first in that study. These High School classmates set out for my scalp, for my conquest and undoing. They seemed to presume, what men usually presume under similar circumstances, that the new comer is unduly ambitious, that he is simply "showing off" because he is new, and that the pace which he has set will not and cannot last. They attacked me on every side; they picked every possible flaw in my work and recitations, and in their zeal they some times found impossible flaws. They laughed; they ridiculed; they studied; they worked valiantly. I kept on. They only stimulated me; they filled me with a most exhilarating feeling for my work. They did for my education what no teacher in the world could have done; they made me study and learn what I had previously supposed I knew. They combined; they attacked first in one subject, then in another. They succored each other clandestinely.

27

But each month and term told for me a better and better story. And before the end of my High School course I had reached that uninteresting point in the career of a winner where his rivals give up and concede him victories which he does not win, and the teachers had often to upbraid my classmates for letting errors go by unchallenged simply because I had made them. But in conquering their admiration I did not lose their love. I had played fair, and they were not slow to appreciate the fact.

And how did I support myself meanwhile? My father gave me what assistance he could afford; wages were poor and there were younger children. And his groceryman was continually telling him that if he were in father's place he would not allow an able-bodied boy to go to school while he himself worked.

And other men? Well, other men praised me; they did not assist me. And perhaps it is better that human nature is constituted so; men will praise a struggler when they have no thought of helping him. Help is very often a doubtful blessing, and sometimes praise is too, and this reflection is a convenient solace to those who would not help. If every person who named me "smart" should have been required by law to give me a nickel I should have had at least no financial troubles.

During my first year in the High School I continued to work on the ferry. But when summer came again, my success was threatened by a new danger; the public-spirited citizens of Little Rock were building a "free bridge" across the Arkansas River from the foot of Main Street, and this bridge was to be opened on the Fourth of July. The famous old ferry that had existed from the foundation of the city was then to die. The passing of the old ferry seemed the passing of a friend. I had usually carried a book on my oarsman's seat so that I could read or study while waiting for passengers; and as I rowed to and fro I had conjugated Latin verbs to the stroke of the oars.

In the face of a free bridge how was I to prepare for the Middle Year of the High School and pursue it during the term?

The Heir of Slaves

V. THE STAVE FACTORY AND THE SAWMILL LUMBER YARD

THERE was a "stave factory" and cooper shop in Argenta for the manufacture of barrels and kegs, and one thing that comes into the process of making the barrel heads is to stack the green boards, when they are first sawed from the blocks, and to construct the stack so that air circulation will dry them. They were piled in polygonal hollow squares by first laying a polygon of the pieces of "headin'" on the ground and then continuing round and round as the stack grew higher, up to fifty or more feet, or as high as the one on the ground who was "pitchin' headin'," could shoot the short boards up through the air to the one on the stack who was "layin' headin'."

Here I secured a position luckily, and I had an experience at "layin' headin'" which I shall never forget, and which forms as integral a part of my mental and moral training as any other thing I ever did or any book I ever studied. I was earning "six bits" or seventy-five cents a day, more money than I had ever received steadily before in my life. When an older person did the work which I was doing he received usually one dollar a day. But I was a boy and schoolboy at that, and this fact, though otherwise and elsewhere exemplary, lowers one's price in a "stave factory." The superintendent would not pay a schoolboy one dollar a day, and I doubt whether he would have hired me at all if he had not supposed that like almost all others I would never return to school after finding a position that paid four dollars and fifty cents a week, for I remember how he swore when I quit at the end of the summer, calling me a young fool for throwing away the opportunity of certain employment for the doubtful blessings of "schooling." And the fact of my receiving a lower wage brought me into disfavor with some of the men who worked about the factory, especially with the man who "pitched headin'" to me.

This man was at one and the same time, about as merry and human and as cruel and brutal a fellow as my brain has ever been able to imagine. And nothing that I shall record here has the least feeling of resentment toward his memory, for I regard him as one of my appointed teachers who, whether he willed it or not, gave me (somewhat against my will, too) a most valuable mental and moral discipline. If I should meet him today, I would shake his hand heartily as one of my benefactors, albeit he tried for weeks and weeks to knock my brains out with pieces of green barrel heading. Usually if a man tries constantly to hurt you and you constantly prevent him, he helps you, advances you in the world, the damages which nature assesses in your favor for the unjust attacks upon your life and character. This man was hard as iron in face and heart; stout as an ox in frame; tireless as a machine in action. His wickedness was simple, straightforward; the only good phase of his character was his honest disclaimer of all goodness. He could preach mock sermons as he worked, almost word for word and sound for sound imitations of some of the noisier preachers of the town. He would sing church songs, plantation songs, ribald songs, keeping time to the rhythm of his iron muscles as he sent the pieces of heading shooting into the air. When his jokes were not coarse they were of a good wit and lightened the burdens of all who worked near him.

This man determined to stop me from working at that factory by catching me off my guard and dealing me a terrible blow with a piece of that heading under the excuse of pitching it in the regular way. I felt his determination from the very first by that defensive telepathy with which Nature endues the mind of hunted animals and especially of a hunted man. I was on my guard. I was equally determined to defeat him without ever saying a word to indicate that I suspected him. I must be alert, with my attention fixed from seven o'clock in the morning till noon, and in the afternoon from one o'clock till six. For a long time he tried to wear me out by keeping the pieces of heading flying at me in such rapid succession that there was not a moment even to look aside. But that plan could not succeed, for my work was lighter than his and my nerve and muscles were good. His determination grew with his defeat. He next tried the scheme of pitching with gentle regularity for long periods of time, then suddenly sending up two or more pieces in rapid succession, the last coming with a force to fell an ox. But I was on my guard and both pieces would sometimes be deftly caught to show my skill and vex the tyrant; or when a particularly murderous shot was fired I might incline my body and let it pass harmlessly by and fall to the ground many yards beyond the stack. At such times he would swear roughly and say that he was not to waste his time pitching heading upon the ground. I would make some reasonable remark, trying never to show, or rather determined never to acknowledge that I understood his aim. He knew well that I understood. I have known him to walk away out of sight and slip back from another direction, without my notice, as he thought, and send a piece of heavy heading hissing through the air. It was always either caught or allowed to pass harmlessly by. I have known him to purchase a water-melon from a passing wagon, burst it and apparently sit down to eat it, when suddenly, towards the top of the stack on which I stood, several pieces of heading would be traveling in swift and dangerous succession. Not once did he catch me off my guard. I overheard him remark to another man that I was as hard to hit as a squirrel.

Ill success never discouraged him; he was as persevering as the devil. All summer he kept up his attack; all summer I kept up my defense. If I experienced any feeling like hatred in the beginning, it was very soon all lost, and I came to look upon the daily action as a *contest* in which it was "up to me" to win.

In September, I returned to school and the superintendent swore. My friend of the summer's battle dealt gently with me in the last week or so; perhaps with honest intentions, but without inducing me to take down my defenses. I came away with no scar or mark, save the blackness of my palms, which the green-oak sap had rendered blacker than the backs of my hands.

During the following school season I helped myself by doing odd jobs on Saturdays and by running errands and cutting wood out of school hours. I learned my lessons while going errands or chopping wood. Many people can remember seeing me go along the public streets with a book open before my face. On a long errand I might commit a whole history lesson to memory. When I was cutting wood I opened my book and propped it against a piece of wood at a convenient distance, with a chip holding the leaves apart, and studied by glances as I swung the ax.

Later in the year I found another means of help. My father was fireman for a sawmill and secured for me the privilege of employing some of my Saturdays on the lumber yards. I was later given the position also of "Sunday watchman" for these mill-yards. This kept me absolutely away from Sunday school and away from the day services of the church, but such things I always accepted as temporary means to an end. All day Sunday I camped alone but with my books. If it was cold I made a fire in the mill office and read, and wrote poems, sometimes satires on the members of some class of the High School with which my class was for the moment at war. If the weather was mild I studied or read out on the lumber piles. I early acquired the habit of getting weeks and sometimes months ahead of my class in the text-books. If a subject was to last all the year, I usually finished it in March. When I again went over the work with the class I enjoyed the peculiar profit which comes from review.

During the summer of 1898, preparatory to my senior year in the High School, I worked as janitor in Keys's Business College for white boys. I used to go early to my work in order to study the various books, practice on the typewriting machines and learn the use of certain athletic tools. Under such circumstances the presumption always lies that the janitor is ignorant; but when the boys found out that I could do their lessons for them and outdo their feats on the punching bag and the horizontal bar, some of them grew cold and distant and others enjoyed the exhibitions of my intelligence much as one might enjoy the cleverness of a Simian in the Bronx Park.

My senior year went on as the others had gone. A reporter for one of the daily papers visited the school that year and found us reading Vergil's "Aeneid." The teacher had me scan or read metrically, and the next day there appeared in that newspaper a statement that the reporter found a negro boy that possessed the language of the Romans although he had the color of Erebus. In that same year also a prominent lawyer who held the office, I think, of attorney-general of the state visited the school and saw and heard some performances in mathematics and Latin, and kindly invited me down to his office to help him convince his law partner that a negro could learn Latin. I went on my missionary journey. After quite an extended hearing from various parts of Cicero and Vergil and a theoretical discussion between the two lawyers about the relative value of "rote-learning," the partner in question acknowledged that he was convinced - always addressing the other lawyer, and never addressing or noticing me any more than one would address the machine whose qualities and capacities were the subject of discussion. He finally said that I might profit somewhat by a college education - and by his partner I was thanked and dismissed. It reminds me of certain great educational gatherings to discuss the education of the negro, where the negro is conspicuous by his enforced absence.

In June of 1899 I was graduated as the valedictorian of my class. This valedictory was the first original address I had ever made; it was forty minutes long. And although that speech was the "apple of mine eye" then, when I think of it now it seems strange to me that I should ever have been allowed to pour forth in that park such a tropical effusion in the presence of the school board and the assembled multitude.

This first graduation, where most men stop, filled me with the greatest desire I have ever experienced for further education. How that mountain of difficulty was climbed shall be related now. The summer immediately following my High School graduation wrote into the story of my life another of those delicious chapters of hard and profitable experience to which I turn and read whenever I am tempted by discouragement.

VI. "YOU CAN HAVE HOPE"

THIS was a truly critical time in my career. I knew that I was not even half educated. I desired to go to college - but how? I thought I should have to work for several years and save the money. But I knew that it is not well to interrupt one's education; a thing that is well started goes more easily if it is not allowed to stop. But necessity is necessity, and I had become used to stooping to conquer before her iron rod. So I took the state teacher's examination and secured a "first grade" license. I could have earned forty or fifty dollars a month at teaching.

I knew that most young men of my acquaintance when they could earn fifty dollars a month felt no further need of school. But I did not fear that such a feeling would ever take possession of me. I had come to have a stout faith; whatever difficulty I met, I believed that in some way I could get over it. If faith ever becomes dangerous, mine had perhaps reached that dangerous point where I felt too literally sure that "I cannot fail if I try." I had kept at school for the eight years past because I felt sure that I could do so. I had never failed to solve a problem in all of my lessons, and I had never tackled one with the feeling that I should fail. Always starting out penniless and ever with some new difficulty in my path, I had earned pennies and pushed my way through school from year to year since my mother died. I had overcome many difficulties, never doubting that I should overcome.

At this time I picked up a dusty, worn book that had come into our family by some accident and had lain unopened for years, I read in it a story which filled me with the feeling that mere empty "faith" that is unaccompanied by constant and *faithful* "works" is a comical and a ludicrous phantom. The story ran that a British scholar named Moore believed in the doctrine of transubstantiation, that *if one believes it,* the bread of the sacrament becomes the actual body and the wine the actual blood of Christ. Erasmus did not believe that doctrine, and so journeyed to England to have a friendly discussion with Moore. They met at table without being introduced, neither knowing who the other was. In that day scholars of different nationalities made Latin their international language. A discussion began on the topic of transubstantiation. Moore, not knowing with whom he was arguing, stood up for the faith; Erasmus, not knowing whom he was opposing, said that he did not believe that faith could transubstantiate matter. Erasmus discovered his opponent through his argument and cried out: *"Aut tu Morus es, aut nullus!"* (Either you are Moore, or nobody.) And Moore with ready wit replied: *"Aut tu es Erasmus, aut diabolus!"* (Either you are Erasmus or the devil.) Then Moore claimed that the doctrine was true for those who *believed* it, and that the act of faith made the fact. And Erasmus, outdone in argument, decided not to be outdone in demonstration, and when he was returning to the continent, he asked Moore to lend him his horse, saying simply that Moore would surely get his horse back. But when he reached his home in Europe, instead of sending back the horse, he sent to Moore the two following stanzas:

> *"Quod mihi dixisti*
> *De corpore Christi:*
> *'Crede quod edas et dis'* -
> *Sic tibi rescribo*
> *De tuo palfrido:*
> *Crede quod habeas et habes."*

And although I have seen neither the book nor the story since, I remember that I made the following mental rendition of those stanzas into English:

> "What you to me have said
> About the sacred bread
> 'Believe it's Christ's body and it's that' -
> So I write back to you
> About your palfrey too:
> Believe that you have it and hav't."

The story impressed me: how was a fellow to get his horse or win his spurs through mere faith without acts? I inquired of

36

my friends if it were not possible for one to work his way in college. The pastor of the First Congregational Church of Little Rock, a graduate of Talladega College in Alabama, offered to write an intercessory letter to that institution if I could permit him to say how much I should be able to pay toward my college expenses in cash - and that was the "rub." But I told him to write for conditions and that I would set to work to earn the required cash. He gave me the address of the president of the school and I also wrote a frank letter. It was now July and I could wait for a reply; I must set to work in the hope of earning an acceptable amount of cash. I entered again upon one of those life experiences which are hard enough in their passage, but which in their recollection verify the truth of Vergil's line, that "perchance some day it will be pleasant to remember even these things."

The new railroad, then popularly known as the "Choctaw," was being built through the wilderness of Arkansas, through sections where neither railroads nor other enginery of civilization had ever gone before. My father was at work on the line forty miles up the Arkansas River, in a tangled jungle only accessible to river boats. Concrete bridges were being built over the streams and gorges, and cuts were being blasted through the hills. It was rough work that only the hardiest men could stand. There is always a chance to secure a position in such work; it is so hard that vacancies are constantly occurring, but the summer was wearing away and I must hurry. I wrote my father that I was coming, and did not wait for his reply, for I knew he would think it impossible for me to do the work.

After journeying a day and a night, working my way on a river steamer among the "roustabouts," I reached the frontier-like scene of a railroad camp. The bulk of the laborers and camp-followers were of the scum of humanity, white and black; there were rough, coarse men and undesirable women. My father tried to act the presumption that I had come to visit him; he studiedly said nothing to me to imply that he had any idea of my attempting that work. I coolly told him of my prospects for going to college, and that I had come to work. I shall never forget the wistful, anxious, half-sad look of his eyes as I took up my spade and wheelbarrow and went "on the grade" among the men. There were shoveling and wheeling of dirt and crushed stone. Concrete mixing machines were not then in use, and the mixing had to be done by the men with shovels - the heaviest, hardest work imaginable. On my first day at concrete-mixing the men laughed and swore that I could not last till noon, but would "white-eye." That term was applied to the actions of the sufferer because his eyeballs rolled in a peculiar manner, showing the white, when he became overheated and fell upon the ground. I did last till noon; and then the foreman, a stocky German of the coarsest possible nature, who had kept a half amused eye on me all the morning, expecting to have some fun when I should "white-eye," was so touched by the determination with which I stuck till noon that he gave me lighter work. At nights I had only vitality enough left to bathe in the green waters of the bayou and lie down to rest in my tent. On Sundays I read two borrowed books, one of them being "Uncle Tom's Cabin." Most of the men gambled all day Sundays and caroused till late at night. My better habits soon gave me superior strength and endurance and I could tire the toughest rival. This seemed wonderful to the men. They seemed to think that I was a strange fellow. They did not reckon on the habits of life.

For about a month I had received no word from the president of Talladega College as to whether my application could be accepted, when one day there came in the steamboat mail a card, bearing the Ohio postmark and signed "G. W. Andrews":

"Your frank and interesting letter has been received. I cannot say definitely now, but write to say you can have hope."

"You can have hope." That was after all a great message at the right time and place. It seemed to anticipate a more definite reply. I worked all summer on that card of "hope." Not another word ever came. In the multitude of the president's duties, and perhaps of similar applications, my case had doubtless slipped from his memory and notes. But I hoped and worked, and worked and hoped. September came and wore away towards

October. No word. But there was "hope." I had heard that
Talladega College was to open on the first Tuesday of October.

Meanwhile my evident intelligence had won for me a little
better position from the good-natured, coarse-spoken German,
and for my last month I was put to assist the cook and keeper of
the commissary boat. My father had returned to the city to
engage in other work. I did not tell the foreman that I was going
to quit and go to school. I knew better, most of my pay was still
due and it would have been all kept and I myself kept for a
period. There was no law in that wilderness but the law of the
jungle. I had seen the foreman man chasing white men with a
revolver, as one might chase rabbits.

On the Saturday before the first Tuesday in October I drew
all my pay and got excused to go to the city, as the men
sometimes did. The steamer was not in, so I had to cross the
river and walk fifteen or twenty miles to the nearest railroad
station. I left at daylight and caught the train at noon.

It was an uncivilized world from which I had escaped, the
only appearance of civilization being from its uglier phase,
leased convicts with their "coon-tail" stripes on a farm in a lone
valley half a dozen miles from the railroad camps. As one
journeyed through the woods he would occasionally come upon
a path which would lead to the hut of poor white people; they
usually had no floor or chairs and slept on rude "bunks" or on
quilts upon the bare ground. It has always appealed more
powerfully to my sympathies to behold poor, degraded white
people than to behold the same class of my own race. I suppose
it is because the degraded white man is such a contrast to the
opportunities and attainments of his race, so that his position
seems to be a real *de*-gradation, and it is a less sad spectacle to
see a man simply *down* than to see a man *downed*.

On Sunday I went to see the Congregational preacher, told
him of the card of "hope," and that I had had no further word. He
concluded that the president had overlooked me, but said that he
had heard that if a worthy student could deposit thirty or forty

dollars with the treasurer he might be given sufficient work to meet the rest of his bills for the year. Examining my accounts I found that I had to my credit about fifty dollars; my fare from Little Rock, Ark., to Talladega, Ala., would be about fifteen dollars; so that I could spend five dollars for some necessary articles and go with the minimum of thirty dollars.

I went. I was actuated by faith and the "hope." It was something of a venture for a boy of eighteen, who had never before left the neighborhood of home and home-folk. But how was one to get his horse unless to faith he should add deeds?

VII. A CHRISTIAN MISSIONARY COLLEGE

I REACHED Talladega at night and went early the next morning to the home of the college president, to try my fate again as I had tried it three years before with the high school authorities in Little Rock. He had forgotten me, but remembered when I mentioned the "card of hope." With the coolness and slowness of one who has prepared to look fate in the face I said: "Not hearing any more from you I decided to come and see. And" - drawing something slowly from my pocket - "and I have here *three ten* dollar bills." I noticed the change in the good man's countenance between the words *three* and *ten*; too often had he faced the difficulty of finding a way for apparently worthy students who brought less than a tenth part of their year's expenses. When he learned that I had come five hundred miles on faith, the smile that lit his countenance was auspicious. My star of "hope" had not misled me. He said that he would give the thirty dollars to the treasurer, and asked if I could hitch a horse, milk a cow and work a garden. I replied that I could learn to do any kind of work.

My faith and adventure evidently made a great impression on this man. In his chapel talk that morning, without calling names or making indications, he told a story to the assembled students, how a young man had written from a distant state; how the correspondence had been lost and forgotten; how the fellow had based his hope on a rather indefinite proposition, had worked hard all summer to earn a few dollars, had come many miles. He described the coolness with which this young man had faced him and his own shifting emotions between the words "three" and "ten."

I had not seen a school test all summer, and in my entrance examinations I learned what an excellent preparation it is *not to prepare* for an examination, but to learn each daily lesson and then take a period of rest and not of cramming just before the test. And for the remainder of my school life I prepared for the

41

examination of tomorrow by retiring at eight or nine o'clock the night before.

First the Latin teacher started in to test me in Cicero, which I read so easily that he closed it and opened Vergil's "Aeneid," asking me to scan and read. I announced that I could read the first six books, and he turned from book to book, forwards and backwards, but I always "scanned and read." I was then passed on to the teacher of

mathematics. Many white people have an honest opinion that the negro mind is characteristically unmathematical. The teacher asked me to draw the figure and demonstrate the proposition that the sum of three angles of a triangle is equal to two right angles. He added that he would go about some desk work and that I might call his attention when I was ready. As a good-natured resentment to this last statement I called his attention at once, drawing the figure "free-hand" as I did so, and announced that I was "ready." It is a simple and easy proposition, and it was so clearly demonstrated that this teacher, who was the college dean, gave me no further examinations and enrolled me in the sophomore class. So I never was a *freshman*.

I noticed that I was not put to milking cows and hitching teams, willing as I was, but was given work in the college library. In the first of January came the annual week "of prayer," and I joined the little Congregational church which is fostered in connection with the college. I was just about nineteen years old. Why had I not become a church member before this time? That is a thing worth explaining in the interest of the younger generation of negroes. I believed in God and the church, and had always been a most faithful worshiper, but I could not dream dreams and see visions. Without dreams and visions no one was allowed to join the average negro church of the past. The cause that produced many of the negro songs was the fact that the candidate was required to bring and sing a "new song" to prove that he was really converted by God, for the doctrine was that "the devil can convert you, but he can't give you a new song." Rather suggestive, this idea of the unpoeticalness of the devil. It

42

would amuse more than it would instruct for me to relate some of the ridiculous stories which I have heard accepted in church as convert's "experiences." At last I had found a church which did not require that I visit hell, like Dante, in a dream, to be chased by the hounds of the devil and make a narrow, hair-raising escape. And I have been a member of this church since my first college year.

Talladega College is a typical monument of unselfishness. There is nothing in the annals of human history that outrivals the unselfishness that founded and has maintained these institutions for half a century. When the institution was founded in 1867 practically the whole negro population was illiterate and penniless. It is on record that many workers gave their services absolutely free. The sentiment of the South was naturally opposed to negro education, especially at the hands of its late enemies. The early workers had to face something more than mere social ostracism: the Ku Klux Klan did not stop with that barbarity of civilization, but often adopted real barbarities, terrifying, banishing, whipping and killing. It is interesting to note what an *evolutionary* influence a school like Talladega has on the sentiment of its neighborhood; white people of the town are now among its chief defenders whenever danger is threatened, and are among its best donors when a new building is to be erected.

And oh, the devolvements of Father Time! The building which has been the main educational hall of the institution for forty years, was erected by slave labor in 1852-53 as a college for white boys. One of the slaves who toiled at the work has since had his many children and grandchildren educated in it.

In my first winter at Talladega I won the college oratorical contest and several other literary prizes. This suggested to the president and faculty the idea of sending me to the North in the following summer with a party of four other students and a teacher on a campaign in the financial interest of the college. The teacher, who has since become President Metcalf, presented the work, the aims and the needs of the institution, the quartet of boys sang and I delivered an address which I prepared especially for the campaign. That speech and that campaign proved to be the doorway of my future, as will appear.

It was in the summer of 1900, and it was my first time north of the Ohio and the Potomac. We went northward in the month of June through Tennessee and Kentucky into Ohio, thence eastward, visiting Niagara and the summer haunts of the rich in the Adirondacks and concluding our campaign in the New England States in September.

It was Commencement time when we reached Oberlin, and the class of 1875 was celebrating its twenty-fifth anniversary. Professor Scarborough of Wilberforce University, the negro scholar who is a member of this class, was present at an impromptu parlor entertainment by the five boys of our party, and he so much liked a recitation which I combined from Spartacus to the Gladiators and The Christian Gladiator that when we parted he gave me in the act of handshaking a silver half dollar. I noticed what he did not notice, that the coin bore the date of "1875," the year of his class - and I have it now, black with age and non-use in my purse.

At Akron, O., an event happened on which hangs a chain of circumstances; the people requested that my speech be printed in pamphlets so that copies could be purchased. Copies were sent to Dr. G. W. Andrews, the head of Talladega College, the author of my "card of hope." He marked a copy and sent it to Dr. A. F. Beard, the senior secretary of the American Missionary Association.

This trip impressed me with the unselfish spirit of the Christian people of the North - and also showed me that the good people of the North had a very inadequate idea of the real capacity of the American negro. When we visited the summer camp of Mr. Harrison, ex-president of the United States, members of his party expressed frank surprise that a party of negro college students could sing and speak and deport themselves so well - and I myself was scrutinized with a most uncomforting curiosity.

Our little campaign paid expenses and brought back a thousand dollars for the college - a small sum of money but a big experience. Moreover I had seen Yale, had actually looked upon its elms, its ivies and its outer walls. From that day the audacious idea began to take me that I must push my educational battles into its gates.

VIII. PREPARING FOR YALE IN IRONWORK

WHEN we reached Talladega after our summer campaign of 1900 I received what was then the greatest surprise of my life, an invitation to speak at the annual meeting of the American Missionary Association to be held in Springfield, Mass., in October. Doctor Beard had read my summer campaign speech, and I was asked to come more than a thousand miles to speak for ten minutes. This invitation gave me my first direct impression of the lofty Christian spirit of the great organization of whose educational work I was a beneficiary. I was a boy of nineteen years, an almost unknown student, and in a position to be commanded. On my way to Springfield I met for the first time Dr. Booker T. Washington, who was likewise invited to speak at the annual meeting. And although the incident has probably never recurred to the mind of that honorable gentleman, I remember that when he learned my mission he shared with me his space in the Pullman car and treated me with such kindly consideration that I was asked by passengers if I was not Mr. Washington's son.

AT THE SPRINGFIELD MEETING

The Court Square Theater was packed, and there was an overflow meeting in the church across the street. My speech was lengthened from ten to about twenty minutes at the suggestion of officials who sat upon the platform, the suggestion being made while I spoke. When I crossed the street to speak at the overflow meeting, Doctor Boynton, who presided, said, "If they do this in the green tree, what will they do in the dry?" The subject of this "green tree" discourse was characteristic of a boy under twenty who had just escaped from the sophomore class, Negro Evolution. But the matter was more practical than the title. And although I have since enjoyed the enthusiasm of many occasions where the speaker and his audience become one-hearted and one-souled, I have never had a more thrilling experience or a more

46

appreciative audience than the one in the Court Square Theater. Yet I had heard that Northern audiences were *cold*.

The summer of 1901 gave me an opportunity to learn more of real Black Belt conditions. I assisted in the summer school work of a Talladega College graduate who founded an institution in a rural community more than ten miles from the nearest railroad station. There the negro population greatly preponderates; the negro owns much of the land; and next to nothing is done by the authorities of the state for public instruction. I was impressed by the humanity, the simplicity and the universal peaceableness of American black folk where they are left practically to themselves.

I finished at Talladega College in 1902. The old problem of further education returned. I refused a position in our High School at Little Rock because I wanted to go to Yale or Harvard. Doctor Andrews, who seemed to have a perfect confidence in my future, was trying to get some person of means to assist me at Yale. Dean Henry P. Wright of Yale, after reading the recommendations of my former teachers, had written that I could enter the junior class. This great scholar and good man has been a constant friend since that first acquaintance.

As in former days, I determined to help myself by some decisive move. Having relatives in Chicago, I thought that I might secure work in a great city like that; and going thither immediately after my graduation I luckily found an opening in Gates's Ironworks on the north side of the city among Poles and other foreigners. I was a "helper," supposed to assist the workmen wherever my services were needed. I was an apparently unwelcome object to the Poles until they found out that I could speak German with them. These members of the Catholic faith were much entertained and amused at my repetitions of German and medieval Latin poems to the swinging of my iron sledge. They sought my company and conversation at noon.

Nine dollars a week for about a dozen weeks will not pay a fellow's bills at Yale for ten months. But I hoped to save enough to reach New Haven and support myself for a week or two, at the risk of finding a chance to earn my board and expenses. Besides, this ironwork gave me superior physical strength, which is a good part of any preparation for college. At night I read Carlyle and Emerson, Latin and German, in anticipation of work at Yale. In the middle of the summer I received a word from Doctor Beard of the American Missionary Association in New York, saying, "I am off for Europe, and when I return in the fall I expect to find you at Yale."

The note of that "expectation" sounded like a challenge, and I redoubled my determination and easily passed by all the huge temptations of a great city. On Sundays I attended Moody's church and the city Young Men's Christian Association. It appeared strange to me that out of 40,000 negroes I saw no other one at this Young Men's Christian Association during the whole summer.

I became acquainted with Paul Laurence Dunbar, the negro poet, who was living in Chicago. He cheered me on and wrote encouraging letters until I had finished at Yale. He said that a course at Harvard had always been the unrealized ambition of his life - and how he had earned his breakfasts a few years before by walking seven miles on the hard pavements of Chicago. I was impressed with the possible consequences to one who has to battle against the sort of social and economic world that is presented to a black boy in the average Northern city. It might destroy his health and injure his morals. There was pathos in Dunbar's constant praise of the fact that I did not touch any kind of strong drink nor any form of tobacco.

With a faith astonishing to remember I left Chicago in September, settled my preliminary bills at Yale and was enrolled as a junior, with fifteen dollars left in my pocket and the necessity of finding work to earn my board and room. I secured work in the roof garden and restaurant of the city Young Men's Christian Association, where I could assist the kitchen force in various sorts of work and wash the windows to earn my board. Board is a large and necessary item.

A few days afterwards there came a letter from Mr. D. Stuart Dodge of New York City saying that he had heard from Doctor Andrews of Talladega College, that I was at Yale, well started, inclosing a check for fifty dollars, and adding that he had one more fifty for my use whenever I should advise him that it was needed. He spoke like a familiar friend, although I had never heard his name before. I put the money in the New Haven Savings Bank and advised the donor, with thanks, that I was earning my board and should certainly not need more money until the beginning of the next term, after Christmas, when tuition bills and new books might bring the need. Something in my letter appealed to the favor of this good man. He sent a second fifty and promised a third fifty upon my request. He read my letter to his aged mother, Mrs. William Dodge, then over ninety years of age, and she insisted that twenty-five dollars additional be sent me on her personal check, with the special direction that it be spent for winter clothes. The thoughtful and sympathetic woman heard that I was from the South. This friend whom I had never seen did even more; he wrote to his cousin, Sec. Anson Phelps Stokes of Yale University and advised him of my presence among the thousands of that institution. Mr. Stokes pleasantly invited me to command his assistance when I needed it. I could have created the need by stopping the process of earning my board, but I instinctively felt that the work was better.

By their unpatronizing spirit through all of this, these people lifted up and established my respect for mankind. They conferred a blessing upon me as if it were a joy to them, and asked to help me as one might request a favor.

Encouraged and edified by such noble spirits at the start I do not now wonder that I reached upward with body and mind and entered upon two of the most interesting and successful years of all my educational career.

IX. YALE - THE HENRY JAMES TEN EYCK ORATORICAL CONTEST

MY FIRST year at Yale was full of experiences for which former school struggles had in a measure prepared me. After the Christmas examinations, when students are graded for the first term's work, I was classed in Grade A, which according to the policy of the Self-Help Bureau exempted me from payment of tuition, and I stayed in Grade A, never paying another dollar of tuition during my years at Yale. Board I could earn, and other expenses I could manage. A room in White Hall was secured by the kindness of Dean Wright, into whose Latin class I had luckily fallen. After Christmas my Yale studentship was no longer an experiment, and I set out with confidence on the run toward June.

Early in the year there appeared on the bulletin ten subjects for the "Ten Eyck Prize" in oratory. Among them was the simple word, "Hayti." The oration is first written and passed in under an assumed name; there were over three hundred men in my class and about thirty-five passed in papers. Of these the judges chose ten to enter the first speaking contest. At this first speaking five are dropped and five advanced to the final contest. The five who are dropped receive the five third prizes. Of the five who are advanced the successful one will receive the first prize and the four will receive the four second prizes.

I decided to win the first prize. It is a bold thing to acknowledge, but such was my decision. I kept my work at the Young Men's Christian Association until I should see my name among the ten. Once among the ten I felt as sure to win the first prize as I had ever felt that I would master the difficulties of a lesson.

About three weeks before the time for the final contest, which was to take place about the first of April, the "ten" were published and my name appeared with the subject Hayti.

The Heir of Slaves

My subsequent plans and decisions seem as audacious to me now as they must to the reader of this narrative. I told my Young Men's Christian Association friends that my name was among the Ten Eyck "ten," and that the first prize would settle my bills for the rest of the year, and that I should win if I gave up extra work and devoted myself to the last three weeks of the contest. "If you do not win," they said, kindly, "you may return." I wrote Doctor Andrews of Talladega College that I was among the ten and that I would be among the "five" at the close of that week. After the preliminary contest I wrote him that I was one of the five and that I would win the first prize two weeks later unless the gods should interfere. I learned later that Doctor Andrews read these missives in public as fast as he received them in the South, and they must have seemed utter audacity to all but him. On April 1 in College Street Hall I was awarded the first prize by the five judges.

My ambition to win was stimulated by a desire to further the acquaintance of other peoples with my race. I had noticed that when I did my classwork among the best, more curiosity was awakened than when a Jew or a Japanese ranked among the best. The surprise with which I was taken struck me as due to a *lack of expectation* in my fellows, and I would succeed in order to cause others to expect more of the American negro.

The negro students were less than one-half of one per cent. of the three thousand men at Yale. The negro might not be expected to win often. But judging from the press and personal comment that followed, it would seem that the whole world was a little too much surprised.

But not all that was said and done was prompted by curious surprise rather than positive appreciation. The next morning I found in the Yale post office a check for fifty dollars with appreciation from the Yale Glee, Banjo and Mandolin Clubs Association. For weeks there came daily twenty-five or more appreciative letters. Mrs. Corinne Roosevelt Robinson, sister of the President, had never quite forgotten me since my little summer campaign speech in 1900, and she sent Godspeed and a personal check. One of the most highly appreciated letters came from ex-Pres. Grover Cleveland. A good lady of Newport gave me my first and only diamond pin. There came through the mails from New York City three fifty-dollar gold certificates in an anonymous letter signed by "An Unknown Well-wisher." It contained half a dozen words, the briefest and the fullest missive ever sent me. I remembered the text that begins "Unto him that hath."

So many good and sensible letters were bound to be offset by some others of more or less eccentric ideas and suggestions. Some organization in Kentucky, which seemed from their literature to have had some designs on Hayti for some time, wrote me a proposal that they would seize the island by some sort of filibustering expedition from the United States if I would accept the presidency. Shades of Dessalines and Toussaint L'Overture! I had no desire to add to the volcanic little government's already too numerous chief executives.

The appreciation of my classmates was generous. When my name was seen among the ten, there was a mixture of amused and sympathetic interest. The proportion of amusement was overdone only by one Jew who was an unsuccessful aspirant for the honor and who referred to me among the boys as "the black Demosthenes." I told him it would have been more Jewlike for him to say black David, or black Jacob. When I entered the five, I was taken more seriously. And when I won the final contest there was a burst of generous and manly enthusiasm.

I never like to describe human ugliness for its own sake, but there was one fellow who is worth describing because he is such a good illustration of a type - not a Yale type, but a type of man. Among the best and seemingly sincerest of my Yale friends were some boys from the South, especially from the freedom-loving hills of the border states. But there was one fellow from the state school of my own state. We entered Yale together and he, knowing me to be a Southern negro fighting for my very existence, was at first very, very patronizing. He would "hello" me a block away, inquire with a half amused, half good-natured smile "how I was making it?" and make every effort of bland superiority. I uniformly and politely accepted all his good advances, never seeking them. Soon my classmates began to talk on the campus about my work. He became less friendly - I had to be nearer to him than the distance of a block to get a "hello." After the Christmas "exams" the boys had tales to tell; how I walked out from nearly every examination when most of them were not half through. Then he hardly spoke when he met me face to face; I tried hard to be uniform and unconscious of change. Next day after the oratorical contest I met him squarely on the street, and as I was about to give the friendly greeting he pulled down his hat over his eyes and passed as one passes a lamp-post.

People naturally ask how I fared during my next year, my senior year, at Yale. A month before my graduation I was invited to address the State Congregational Association of Illinois, and when a minister of that body asked me that question I told the story of a negro woman in the south who believed in "voodooism." Her husband was fussy and disagreeable, so she went to the "conjure doctor" to get a remedy for the old man's distemper. The conjurer gave her a bottle of clear liquid, and directed that when the "fuss" started in the house she must take a mouthful of it herself, and added his particular direction that it must not be swallowed under a quarter of an hour after being taken into the mouth. She followed directions and the vicarious treatment completely cured the old man. Returning to the doctor in astonishment she asked what the remedy could be, and he replied: "Cold water - but it kept *your* tongue still!"

But there is nothing more generous and noble than the heart of a boy, and young men are but "boys grown tall." During my senior year they acknowledged my right to a part of their world. They never quite got away from the surprise that "you do your lessons as well as anybody!" While crossing the campus at examination times I was often stopped by a crowd of fellows who had just finished some examination. They would hand me the list of questions, and as I answered them they would say, "I made it," or "I failed," according as their answers had agreed or

53

disagreed with mine. "Pickens, you ought to be a lawyer!" shouted one fellow after I had gone through such a list of questions from our five-hour law course. I could hardly have registered to vote in that fellow's state.

At graduation time I was ranked in the "Philosophical Oration" group of the class who are credited with "honors in all studies." I had been with the class two years, just the time required to merit a Phi Beta Kappa Key if one's scholarship warrants it. So much was printed and said about my admission to this society that a clear statement might correct some error. It was said that my admission was opposed. Well, a great university is much like the outside world; it holds many different spirits. No one should be surprised at differences of opinion in a *university*. In our senior year a resolution was introduced in the Phi Beta Kappa Society that no one be admitted to membership that year except such as began as Freshmen. I entered Yale as a Junior; but there is no way of determining that this was a "grandfather clause" inspired by my presence. A few fellows tried mischievously to impress me that the legislation was in my honor, but I consistently and persistently refused to acknowledge it - and somehow the resolution proved ineffective and I was awarded a key. The Phi Beta Kappa Society is based on scholarship, and Yale is a very democratic community.

AFTER-WORD

After Yale, what? A famous lecture bureau of New York City laid before me a tempting contract to be carted around over Europe and America for three years as a sort of lecture-curiosity. I had been invited to speak before various dignified gatherings, at Newport, Hartford and at the annual banquet of the Citizens' Trades Association of Cambridge, Mass. But after seeking and finding good advice in the secretary of Yale University, the secretary of the American Missionary Association and Paul Laurence Dunbar who had tried the curiosity-show business, I decided that show-lecturing would be of doubtful influence on my future - although it would have given me an opportunity to accomplish one of the desires of every college man, a visit to the Old World.

The work of education seemed to offer a greater field of usefulness to a negro than any other profession. My own school struggles emphasized this thought. Back to the South was my inclination. That section is big with the destiny of the American negro, and therefore with the future of the negro race in the whole world. After considering the timely offers of various educational authorities, including those of Tuskegee and the American Missionary Association, I decided to begin work in the American Missionary Association College at Talladega, Ala., where I have been teacher of languages since leaving Yale in 1904. My experience of the usefulness of this institution, as well as gratitude for the greatest of benefits, made this decision logical and good.

On my way from New England to Talladega a visit to the World's Exposition in St. Louis brought me by Little Rock, Ark., and the scenes and memories of public-school days, the "skiff-ferry" and the "stave factory" - and the colored citizens and a few white friends gave me the biggest and most pleasant reception of all my life.

In the last six years it has been impossible for me to supply all the demands upon my energies as a lecturer or speaker at institutions and gatherings. I have visited nearly all of the important negro schools of the South, and it has given me a good look into the condition and needs of my people. In 1906 I took up Esperanto, and after a correspondence with Esperantists all over the world, I was awarded a diploma by the British Esperanto Association. In 1908 Fisk University honored me with the degree of Master of Arts.

In 1905 I met the most helpful and the most enduring good fortune of all my life, the traditional and the real "best woman in the world." Miss Minnie Cooper McAlpine who like myself was a product of the American Missionary Association work, had graduated at Tougaloo University in Mississippi and taught for three years in the American Missionary Association school at Meridian. Since this meeting there have come in succession three of the brightest and best joys that high heaven lends to earth, William, Jr., Hattie Ida and Ruby Annie.

These latter years have a history of their own - which can be better written, perhaps, when they are seen through a perspective of years. Had I written of my boyhood experiences right on the heels of their passage, I could not have presented them in their truer light and proportion. The distance of years lends not merely enchantment but sobriety to the view.

To advance your life is but to push forward the front of your battle to find the same inspiriting struggle still. Oh, the blessing of a boyhood that trains to endurance and struggle! To do the best one can, wherever placed, is a summary of all the rules of success. When I was in the public school of Argenta, Ark., I one day missed a word in the spelling class, the only word I missed during the five years, and a word that I could easily have spelled. The teacher took quick advantage of the careless trick of my brain and passed the word on to my neighbor without giving me the usual second trial, saying as he did so that a boy who had never missed a word had no right ever to miss a word. He wished, no doubt, to punish carelessness. That one missed word was more talked of among my fellows than all the hundreds of words I had spelled, and I was taught the lesson that the man who succeeds is never conceded the right to fail.

I have learned that righteousness and popularity are not always yoke-fellows, and sometimes run a contrary course. From early boyhood I was laughed at among my fellows for the contemptible weakness of totally abstaining from strong drink and tobacco, while in my manhood the best of my fellows commend the abstention as a virtue. I have learned the uplifting lesson that the real heart of humanity appreciates manhood above things; as a copperless struggler I was often accorded a place above the possessor of gold. I have been impressed, not that every single thought and deed in the world is good, but that the resultant line of humanity's movement is in the direction of righteousness, and that human life and the world are on the whole good things.

HISTORIC
PUBLISHING

2015
**"Dedicated to the accurate and
Historical integrity of classic works"**

www.ingramcontent.com/pod-product-compliance
Lightning Source LLC
Chambersburg PA
CBHW071330310526
45789CB00017B/2164